ISBN: 87191-217-1
Library of Congress Catalog Card Number: 72-85041

Sea Lion Island

JULIAN MAY

Illustrated by Fred M. Irvin

Creative Educational Society, Inc., Mankato, Minnesota 56001

The big bull sea lion was heading for home. He swam southward for hundreds of miles—all the way from the coast of Oregon to the little Channel Islands that lay off southern California. He was a huge animal, seven and a half feet long and weighing nearly 600 pounds. He was eight years old, in the prime of life. This year he would be a beachmaster, one of the rulers of Sea Lion Island.

He swam swiftly, pushing himself along with his strong webbed feet. When he was hungry, he uttered strange clicking sounds underwater. The sound bounced off schools of squid or fish and returned to his small ears. The natural "sonar" helped him locate food, even at night or when the water was murky.

The Pacific waters were cold but his hairy coat and thick
layer of blubber kept him warm. Sometimes heavy fog spread
over the waters, hiding the shore. But he was never lost.
A natural compass within his brain would guide him to his
home island, to the beach where he was born and where he
would find his mates.

It was late January as he swam through the Santa Barbara Channel—almost home. He passed far to the west of oil platform A-21, which stood on stilts five miles offshore. He knew nothing about the men who worked on it, pumping oil from beneath the sea bottom. Nor did he know that something terrible had just gone wrong. The oil well under the sea had just blown out. Bubbles of gas and heavy black crude oil were pouring out into the sea.

The bull sea lion, unaware, hauled his huge body onto
the shore of his home island. He barked noisily, telling
the other bulls that he had arrived. He waddled clumsily
to a group of cow sea lions that lay resting on the beach.
They looked at him in a bored manner. Barking constantly,
he moved around the group of cows. He was claiming them
as his mates, and his barking told other bulls to stay away.

The little spot of beach became his territory. The smaller, younger males were allowed to enter it if they didn't bark and challenge the beachmaster. But a barking male was asking for a fight. Sometimes the big bull went lunging at a rival, slashing at the other bull with his sharp tusks. He received some wounds in these fights, but none were serious. Other beachmasters gathered their own groups of females. The younger, weaker bulls had none.

On the oil platform, men worked day and night to stop the leak. But the thick, black liquid rose up to the surface and spread for miles in every direction. Sea birds that dived through the oil slick were coated with poisonous goo. Some died at once. Others, unable to fly, floated helplessly to the California shore. There people picked them up and tried to save their lives.

Winds kept the oil away from the big bull's island, which
was more than 30 miles from platform A-21. Every day, more
and more California sea lions arrived. Many males came
from the north. Most of the females had spent the winter
in southern waters. But now they had all returned to the
island of their birth. Each female had a pup within her
body, ready to be born. Each mature bull was driven to seek
mates, and from the matings would come next year's pups.

All through the day, the big bull sea lion kept watch over his piece of beach. Sea lion cows slept, basked in the sun, scratched, and groomed themselves. Each evening, they went into the water to feed. The bull patrolled the waters nearby and did not return to shore until the last female was safely landed for the night.

The winds blew strong and the seas ran high. Men worked
at oil platform A-21, trying to plug up the leaking well.
But the oil continued to boil up and spread its coat of
death over the sea. It covered hundreds of square miles
of water and slopped up onto the beaches and rocks. The
oil slick reached the Channel Islands nearest to the mainland.
But the big bull's island was still clean and untouched.

Eleven days after the well blew, the workers managed to seal it up with cement. The oil stopped flowing. But then the sea bottom nearby cracked open and more oil began to spill out. The porpoises, with their large brains, knew that the oil was dangerous. Most of them fled. But a few, young or foolish, swam into the slick. The oil filled their breathing holes and they were smothered.

Most of the fishes and deep-water animals were not harmed. But creatures that lived in shallow water near the shore were coated with oil. Sea anemones, sea urchins, starfish, crabs, mussels, barnacles—they took the poisonous oil into their bodies as they breathed and fed. And they died.

The sea lions took their ease on their lonely island. They fed mostly on squid, but also took octopus and fishes such as anchovy, herrings, and hake. The older animals did not stay long at sea. The yearlings, more playful and not bothered by the problems of breeding, chased each other merrily through the waters—leaping and diving.

Stormy weather came, hindering the men who were trying to
stop the oil leaks and those who attempted to clean up the
mess. The sea lions didn't mind the rain. It kept flies
and other pests from bothering them. Sea gulls wheeled
over the beach, uttering their creaky cries, as the gray
mists closed in and hid the black flood that came closer
and closer to the island.

April came, then early May. Another group of sea lions began to come up on the beach. These were Steller sea lions, more than twice the size of their California cousins and paler in color. They spent most of their time in northern waters. But during the breeding season they came swimming back to have young and to mate. Steller and California sea lions all mixed together on the beach, living fairly peacefully.

The island, far out in the Pacific Ocean, had other members of the seal family as well, although these did not share the same beaches. There were gigantic elephant seals, the males weighing up to four tons and having trunk-like snouts. And there were two kinds of fur seal— the northern or Alaska fur seal and the Guadalupe seal, which migrated northward from Mexico. In addition, smaller harbor seals lived around the island all through the year.

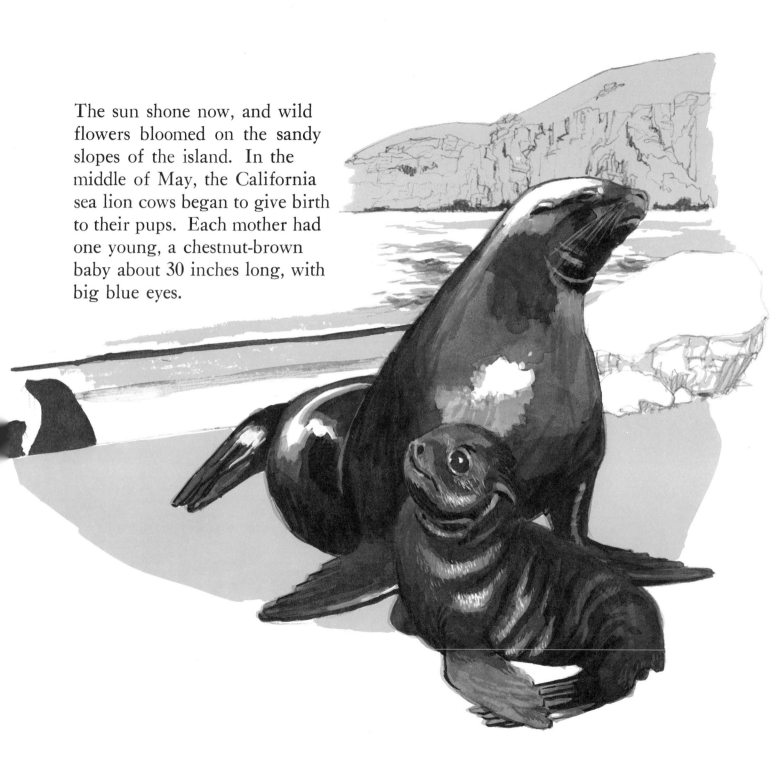

The sun shone now, and wild flowers bloomed on the sandy slopes of the island. In the middle of May, the California sea lion cows began to give birth to their pups. Each mother had one young, a chestnut-brown baby about 30 inches long, with big blue eyes.

The little ones were fed with rich milk from their mothers' bodies. Late in the day, the cows would leave the pups in order to feed. But they always found the right baby again. Each cow knew her own pup's special smell.

The first patches of oil began to reach the island in mid-May, about the time that the first pups were born. The oil on the water glinted green and yellow and had a rainbow sheen. But when it reached the shore it piled up in a thick, black scum several inches deep. The big bull sea lion, who was an intelligent animal, knew that there was something bad about the oil. He herded his group of mates and their babies inland and would not let the cows enter the water.

But they could not stay on land for long. The cows were hungry, not having the thick layer of body fat possessed by the bull. And they felt hot, dry, and itchy. One by one, they slithered down through the thick strip of oil and plunged into the sea. When they returned, they were stained with oil and smelling from it.

On the mainland, men with steam hoses and scrubbers were cleaning up the soiled California beaches. They threw straw in the water to soak up the oil, then took the black straw away. Out in the channel, huge machines like vacuum cleaners sucked floating sludge from the sea's surface. But still the cracks in the ocean bottom leaked oil, and the winds and current carried it to the islands.

The sea lions could not leave their breeding place. Instinct made them stay and raise their young on the beaches where they, themselves, had been born. When the sea lion pups were about ten days old, it was time for them to learn to swim. They did this by themselves, paddling around in the shallow tide pools among the rocks. Some pups found pools of clean water. Others flopped into pools thick with oil. Many of these babies took the poisonous oil into their bodies and died.

As the babies entered the water and became oil-stained, they lost their special smell. Some of the younger, less-intelligent cows failed to know their pups when they returned to nurse. And in this way, a few more babies died. Some of the young adults had perished, too, after frolicking heedlessly in the oil-coated waves instead of spending most of their time on the beach as the older animals did.

Across the channel, at oil platform A-21, men were pouring
tons of sand over the leaking cracks, slowly burying them.
Less and less oil was spilling out. There were no more
vast oil slicks near shore. What was left floated out to
sea, among the islands.

The sun of early summer was hot on the beaches. The big bull sea lion, his coat stained with black, still guarded his territory faithfully. Most of his mates had survived the oil, but nearly half the pups had died as they tried to swim in tar-covered pools. The survivors were growing quickly, their eyes changing from blue to brown.

One day men landed on the island, to take
pictures and see what damage the oil had done.
The big bull sea lion barked a warning
and plunged into the sea. His cows followed—
some carrying their pups by the scruff of the
neck. Only the newborn babies were left,
with their mothers, together with the sea lions
that were too sick to flee.

There were many long caves among the island rocks, carved by the pounding waves. The big bull swam to one of these. It was a good place, around on the other side of a rocky point. The oil had not reached it. Under the water, he barked. His mates heard him and followed him inside.

It was a quiet place, except for the tinkle of water dripping from the roof. A few sea birds had nests in the walls. Green light, coming mostly from underwater, lit the wet rocks. The bull climbed slowly up on a wide shelf at the end of the cave. His mates followed, boosting the pups out of the water. Then the sea lion family rested.

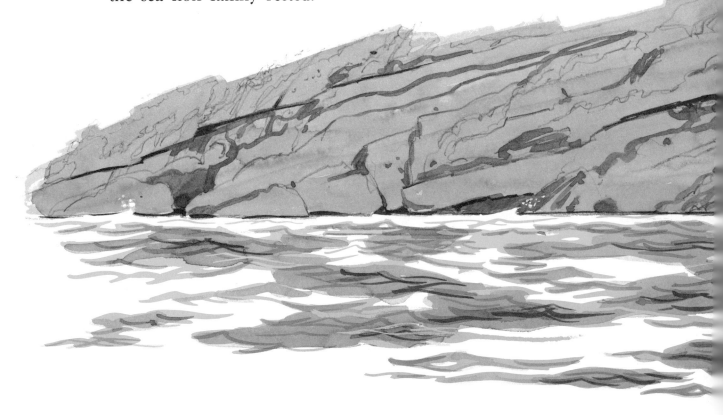

Miles away, on the oil platforms, the pumps were at work
again lifting oil out of the rocks beneath the sea. Most of
the mess had been cleaned up on the mainland. People were
glad to put it out of their minds. Some 4,000 sea birds had
died—but no one had been able to count all the dead sea lions.
The ravens, scavenger birds, had picked their bones and the
bones had sunk into the sand.

The big bull and his family did not
return to the oil-soaked beach.
Through summer and fall, they stayed
near the cave. As they shed their
coats and grew new ones, the oil-
soaked hair was cast away. Half of
that year's crop of pups had perished.
But the big bull had already mated
with the cows, and within each female
a new speck of life was growing . . .
the pup that would be born next year,
when they all came back to Sea Lion
Island.

ABOUT SEA LIONS

The California sea lion is a very intelligent animal, the "trained seal" of circuses and marineland shows. It breeds along the Pacific Coast from middle California to Baja California, Mexico. In winter, some males travel as far north as British Columbia. Males grow up to eight feet long and weigh up to 600 pounds. Females are more slender, up to six feet long and weighing 200 pounds.

The California sea lion looks dark when wet and barks noisily on the beach. Closely related Steller or northern sea lions are much larger, golden brown in color, and fairly quiet.

These animals are told from the true seals (such as the harbor and elephant seal) by their small external ears and their ability to turn their flippers forward and walk on land.

True seals have only a hole leading to the inner ear; they must wiggle on their bellies in order to move on land.

This book is based on a true incident, the Santa Barbara oil spill of 1969, in which more than three million gallons of crude oil gushed into the sea, staining an area of about 800 square miles. The incident caused a public outcry against offshore oil drilling which still continues.

One scientific study showed that not too much damage to the environment resulted from the spill. But other scientists pointed out that damage on the Channel Islands, where there are very few people, was not fully studied. Today the islands are clean again and the sea lions and seals live in peace—until the next oil spill.